Please Note!

This is an emulation of the original book as it appears on Kindle. For this reason, it purposely breaks some conventions of printed books.

From Word to Kindle

Getting Started	3
1 First Steps	7
Working with Word	8
Document Setup	10
Text Cleanup	14
2 Kindle Formatting	19
Special Characters	20
Font Formatting	26
Paragraph Styles	30
Paragraph Spacing	33
Paragraph Justification	37
Line Breaking	40
Page Layout	50
3 Special Elements	55
Other Paragraphs	56
Lists	60
Tables	62
Text Boxes and Sidebars	63
Footnotes and Endnotes	65
Pictures	66
4 Navigation	71
Web Links	72
Internal Links	74
Tables of Contents	77
Menu Items	80
5 Final Steps	83
HTML Export	84
Book Covers	89
Book Data	91
Submitting and Previewing	96

FROM WORD TO KINDLE

Self Publishing Your Kindle Book
with Microsoft Word, or Tips on
Designing and Formatting Your Text
So Your Ebook Doesn't Look Horrible
(Like Everyone Else's)

By Aaron Shepard

Shepard Publications
Friday Harbor, Washington

Aaron Shepard is a foremost proponent of the *new* business of profitable self publishing, which he has practiced and helped develop since 1998. Unlike most authorities on self publishing, he makes the bulk of his living from his self-published books—not from consulting, speaking, freelance writing, or selling publishing services. He lives in Friday Harbor, Washington, in the San Juan Islands, with his wife and fellow author, Anne L. Watson.

The Kindle Publishing Series
From Word to Kindle ~ Pictures on Kindle ~
HTML Fixes for Kindle

The Print on Demand Series
Aiming at Amazon ~ POD for Profit ~ Perfect Pages

And More
The Business of Writing for Children

**For updates and more resources,
visit Aaron's Publishing Page at
www.newselfpublishing.com**

Getting Started

One of the most common ways to prepare Kindle books, and one of the most highly recommended by Amazon, is with Microsoft Word. That's because this familiar word processor provides convenient control over most simple formatting on the Kindle.

Here's the basic procedure:

1. Properly format a Word document and insert links and bookmarks for navigation.

2. Export from Word to HTML—the basic language of Web pages and ebooks.

3. Upload your HTML file to Amazon for Kindle conversion and previewing.

It's not hard to find instructions on this procedure around the Web and in books on Kindle publishing—but these instructions are usually less helpful than they could be. Many, for example, proclaim that Word's HTML output requires extensive alteration and cleanup before you submit it.

This advice is misguided. Some who offer it have drawn their conclusions after simply choosing the wrong export option. Others fuss about a moderate amount of excess code, not realizing that it doesn't increase file size enough to matter or that the Kindle ignores it anyway.

Other instructions will imply the opposite: that conversion is straightforward and just what you would expect. Supposedly, as long as you start with a properly formatted Word document, you'll wind up with a well-formatted ebook. Well, it doesn't really work that way—not without a few techniques for tricking or bullying the Kindle into doing what you want.

Here, then, I offer my own tips for moving a document from Word to Kindle. While the conversion is not as simple and straightforward as some would suggest, it is easy and effective enough that I have used it successfully for over a dozen of my own ebooks—and have received praise for their formatting.

But you can judge the results for yourself. If you're reading the Kindle version, this ebook was produced with the same techniques described here and in my follow-up books, *Pictures on Kindle* and *HTML Fixes for Kindle*. If you're reading a PDF or print version, you're looking at a rough simulation of the ebook's appearance on Kindle.

If you're reading an EPUB version, chances are less that you'll see exactly what I intend. But in Apple's iBooks app, you can at least get closer. On your iOS device, go into the Settings app, scroll to the iBooks settings, and turn off both Full Justification and Auto-hyphenation.

Please note that this book is *not* meant as a comprehensive guide. Among other things, I'm not trying to teach everything you can accomplish on the newer Kindles. Instead, I focus on what will work on *any* Kindle—or at least do no harm. My goal here is design that's competent and reliable, not fancy.

All my instructions are based on Word versions from 2003/2004 to 2010/2011, though earlier and later versions may work as well. If you have a choice of versions, I recommend 2003/2004, in which Word reached its peak. (But 2004 won't run on up-to-date Macs, so the next best choice is 2011.)

The variety of versions I cover means I can't know exactly where a command might be found in your particular version of Word. That's what Word Help and software manuals are for! Anyway, when using Word for something as complex as publishing, you should always have a comprehensive manual on hand.

Of course, Word is not the only word processor that can export HTML for a Kindle book. You can certainly try a different program, but just be aware that my instructions may not apply in every detail. Also keep in mind that Amazon's Kindle converter has been tuned to HTML coming from Word—so the quirks of code from other word processors may not be handled as gracefully.

For updates and related materials, please visit my Publishing Page at

www.newselfpublishing.com

While there, be sure to sign up for my email bulletin, so you'll know when I have anything new, including revisions of this book. And though I'm not able to provide technical support or consulting, I'm always glad to receive comments, as well as suggestions on how my books might be improved.

One final bit of advice before we get to work: No matter what you do, text in a Kindle book will never look as good as it can in print. So, use this guide to make your text as professional as possible, and then let it go. Otherwise, the Kindle will just make you crazy.

Take it from one who has learned the hard way.

1
First Steps

Working with Word

You'll find formatting easier if you make Word display formatting marks that are normally invisible—like paragraph marks. To do this, adjust Word's Display or View options, or just click the Show/Hide button on your ribbon or toolbar. That's the one with the paragraph mark, or *pilcrow* (¶).

●

To keep control of your document, turn off most of Word's automatic formatting and correction. In Word for Windows, go to File > Options > Proofing > AutoCorrect Options. On the Mac, go to Tools > AutoCorrect. On the AutoCorrect tab, turn off any correction you don't need. Do the same on the Math AutoCorrect tab.

In the same dialog box, go to the AutoFormat As You Type tab. I recommend turning off *everything* under "Apply as you type" and "Automatically as you type." Under "Replace as you type," leave on the "smart quotes" option but consider whether you need the others. If you've ever had trouble with Word adding unwanted hyperlinks, this is where to turn that off.

●

To greatly simplify working with styles, be sure to turn off the Editing option "Keep track of formatting." This will prevent Word from creating a new style every time you apply direct formatting. Very important for maintaining sanity!

The location of this option varies in different versions of Word. In Word 2010 for Windows, for example, find it at File > Options > Advanced > Editing Options. In Word 2011 for Mac, it's at Word > Preferences > Authoring and Proofing Tools > Edit.

●

Since 2007, Microsoft has been pushing the Ribbon as a tool for easier formatting. It may or may not be such, but to harness the full power and flexibility of Word, you need to work with dialog boxes. Most of the time in this book, I'll be referring to commands in these dialogs. (They are generally pretty much alike on Windows and Mac.)

On Windows, you can usually access the dialog boxes through the small icons at the lower right corners of the Ribbon's command groups. On the Mac, you still reach them through the menus.

●

It's a sad fact that long-time and advanced users of Word sometimes have more trouble with the program than new users do. That's because of the accumulation of outdated features and settings in your files. If you have odd problems when modifying a document created in an older version of Word, try copying everything *except* the final paragraph mark and pasting into a new, empty document.

If you find that Word for the Mac crashes a lot, use the Mac's Font Book app to locate and discard any older or duplicate sets of Microsoft fonts on your computer. Then delete Word's font cache with a maintenance utility like Marcel Bresink's TinkerTool System (not to be confused with his more basic utility, TinkerTool).

www.bresink.com

Document Setup

Set up your book as a single file. Word can easily handle a book of almost any size in this way. Especially avoid using Word's Master Documents feature, which can cause corruption.

•

Change your document margins and/or page setup to roughly emulate a Kindle page. Though not essential, this will help you gauge your formatting. Currently, I'm roughly emulating Kindle for iPad, with a page size of 6 × 8 inches. My top and bottom margins are 1 inch, and left and right margins are .75 inch, for a type column of 4.5 × 6 inches.

Do *not* adjust your overall document margins by applying left or right indents to your paragraphs! This will narrow your text on the Kindle, not just in Word!

Headers and footers will just be ignored when you export to HTML, so you can include them or not, as convenient.

As an alternative, you could ignore *all* these settings and just switch to Web Layout View. As I'll explain later, this can simplify working with pictures. The main disadvantage is that this view will not show your added page breaks.

•

Any means of starting a new page in Word will carry over to your Kindle book. So, you can insert a manual page break or a section break, whether defined as "New page," "Odd page" or "Even page". Or you can format the first paragraph of a new page with the setting "Page break before." Such formatting could even be added to a style like "Heading 1" for an automatic page break before each new chapter.

One problem with using manual page breaks and section breaks: In Word's exported HTML, the code for these causes *some* Kindles to add a blank line to the top of the page. This might not matter to you—in fact, you might prefer it. But for spacing that's tightest and most *consistent* across Kindles, stick to formatting with "Page break before."

●

Most Kindles will hyphenate words only in the most extreme cases. So, to better emulate Kindle text, leave off hyphenation for your document.

●

If you plan to create preview files with the desktop Kindle Previewer, make sure the document title is correct in the Document Properties or Summary Info. The Previewer will use this title as the book's header. But you don't need to bother with this if your preview file will be created at Amazon KDP. In that case, the header is created from the title you enter in the online form. (If you don't understand about preview files, don't worry. I'll explain them later.)

●

The way print books have evolved, the main text may be surrounded by a good deal of supporting information—title page, table of contents, list of books by the author, book identifiers and classifications, earlier editions, dedication, acknowledgements, preface, foreword, index, glossary, bibliography—you name it. Generally, this extra information is seen as a bonus, and if readers aren't interested, they can always skip over it easily.

On the Kindle, too, the front matter can be skipped—and in fact, Amazon makes that the default, by making most books open where the main text begins. (I'll talk more about that later.)

The main problem arises when Amazon customers want to preview the book, either on Amazon itself or in a downloaded sample. The previewed pages include a percentage of the complete book, and that's normally starting from the beginning. If the front is loaded with extra material, customers will have a harder time reaching the pages that could make the sale, and they'll see less when they get there.

Because of this, many Kindle publishers believe that most front matter should be moved to the back of the book. Unfortunately, this move just creates another problem. On some Kindles, Amazon follows the last page of the book with a special page soliciting reviews and offering related titles for sale—including yours. The more back matter in the book, the less likely that readers will reach that page.

This raises a question: How much of this front and back matter does the book actually need? Dedication? Not really. Info about earlier editions? Probably not. ISBN? It serves no purpose inside the book. Bibliography? That can go on my Web site, if it's needed at all. Index? There are no pages to refer to, and the text can be searched directly!

So, I've gradually pared my front and back matter. At this writing, most of my books have no back matter at all. For front matter, I try to limit myself to a title page, a table of contents, and one page about myself and my other books. For a recent children's picture book, I began with a title page and nothing more.

The truth is, few people care about all that on a throwaway item like an ebook. So, I now save the luxury of extensive front and back matter for the more elegant and leisurely medium of the printed book.

●

You may find it useful to create and maintain a Kindle book template with all book elements, settings, and styles in place, and then paste much of your text into a copy of that. If so, make sure the names of the styles for your pasted text match the style names in your template. Otherwise, Word will add the new styles, which can be confusing.

Also, when copying from another Word document, never include the final paragraph mark! If you do, you'll be adding the document's unused styles as well as all used ones.

Text Cleanup

Much necessary text cleanup can be handled with the Find and Replace dialog box. (In recent Word versions, get to it by choosing Advanced Find.) Click the "More" button or a down-pointing arrow in that box to get to the Special and Format menus. To remove something, specify it in Find but leave the Replace box empty.

●

In the old days of typewriters, typists would indent each paragraph with a series of spaces or a tab. Unfortunately, many people persist in this practice today, instead of simply providing an indent setting as part of paragraph formatting. If you're one of those people, all those multiple spaces and tabs will have to come out.

Tabs can be located with the Special menu of the Find and Replace dialog. For multiple spaces, in the Find box, type the number of spaces you use for indenting.

Another typewriter holdover is typing two spaces between sentences. This looks all right with the typewriter's uniform-width or *monospace* characters but not with the variable-width or *proportional* fonts normally used on the computer and in books. To get rid of double spacing, type two spaces in the Find box, and a single space in the Replace box. (In HTML, multiple spaces are normally collapsed down to one automatically, but Word outputs them in a way that prevents this.)

•

Two other typewriter holdovers have to do with Returns. Unless you're typing something like poetry or a list, a Return should be used only to end a paragraph, not to end a line within it. If you have unneeded mid-paragraph Returns, they'll all have to be deleted. (Sorry, there's no good automated way to do it.)

Space between paragraphs is another improper use of the Return—as we'll discuss later, you get better results from paragraph format settings of Spacing Before and After. To get rid of the extra Returns, you'll need "Paragraph Mark" from the Special menu, inserting it twice in the Find box and once in the Replace box. If you have more than two in a row, just keep running the operation till all consecutive Returns are gone.

•

There are many kinds of characters and formatting that are proper in a Word document but that will not work in a Kindle book and may even cause major problems. Though I will discuss some of these again later, here is a quick list of things that need to be removed or replaced.

• Tabs.
• Optional Hyphens.
• Nonbreaking Hyphens.
• Local adjustments to Character Spacing.
• Local adjustments to Line Spacing.
• Manual Line Breaks (Shift-Return) to control line length. (They're OK if paragraph is centered.)
• Page numbers inserted anywhere but in a header or footer.

• Any fancy layout features like borders, text boxes, columns, or text wrapping around pictures.

Index entries and other hidden text can be left in place or removed, as convenient. Depending on your version of Word, your exported HTML either won't contain that text or will make it invisible. In any case, it won't show up on a Kindle.

•

One product of Word's automatic formatting that you must remove is particularly tricky: the horizontal line. If you've followed my recommendations, you've already turned off the setting that produces these—"Borders" or "Border Lines" in AutoFormat As You Type. But since it's actually a border instead of a normal line, it can't just be deleted.

Instead, place your cursor just *above* the line. In Word for Windows, go to Home > Paragraph, and from the drop-down Borders menu, choose "No Border". On the Mac, go to Format > Borders and Shading. Make sure you're on the Borders tab (not Page Border), then click "None" and "OK."

If you want to replace the deleted line with something that *will* work in your Kindle book, place your cursor on a centered, unindented paragraph and choose "Horizontal Line" from the same drop-down menu or dialog box. This inserts a line graphic that Word will later replace with HTML code. For a sample, see my later discussion of footnotes and endnotes.

•

Your text may have worse intruders if it comes from a program other than Word—especially if you copied the text directly from within that other program. Invisible code or characters can wreak havoc with your Word document, while also being extremely difficult to locate.

If you have the original program, the best approach is to export the document from it in a text-based format that still retains formatting, like Rich Text Format (RTF) or HTML. Then use Word's Insert File command, or else open the file in Word and then cut and paste from there.

If you *don't* have the original program, or if there's only a small bit of text to deal with, you might resort to what Mark Coker calls the Nuclear Option: Paste the text into a text editor or code editor that will automatically discard formatting and invisible elements. (On the Mac, I use BBEdit.) You can then cut and paste from there into Word. The disadvantage is that you lose *all* formatting, including italics, which can be a major nuisance.

●

If, after cleaning up everything you can think of, there's still something screwing up your output, here's how to locate it: First make a copy of the document just for testing. Then delete parts of the text, testing for the problem at each step, till you have it pinpointed.

For instance, you can start by deleting half the document. If the problem disappears, undo that deletion and delete only a quarter; or if the problem persists, delete half of what's left. You should be able to narrow it down quickly.

2
Kindle Formatting

Special Characters

Use book punctuation instead of plain-text, "typewriter" punctuation. Most important is to use "smart quotes" or "curly quotes" (' ' " ") instead of straight ones (' "). This applies to apostrophes, single quotation marks, and double quotation marks. (The apostrophe is usually identical to a single quote when straight, and to a single *closing* quote—the one coming *after* the quoted text—when curled.)

Word will convert your quotes automatically if you have "smart quotes" turned on in AutoFormat As You Type. But you might still see straight quotes in text that you typed with that setting turned off, or that you inserted from another source, like the Web. If so, you can fix them with the AutoFormat command after checking its own setting for this. Note that there are separate settings for AutoFormat and AutoFormat As You Type, so you should turn on "smart quotes" in *both* places.

Another way to fix straight quotes is with Find and Replace. First check that the "smart quotes" setting is turned on in AutoFormat As You Type. Next, type a *straight* apostrophe into *both* the Find box *and* the Replace box, and then Replace All. Word will find each apostrophe or single quote in your document—straight *or* curled—and replace it with one that's automatically curled. Finally, do the same for double quotes.

If you don't want to mess with Word's automatic formatting, you can insert smart quotes manually. The key combinations are listed on the Special Characters tab of Word's Symbol dialog box.

Be aware that automatic formatting may in some cases curl a quote in the wrong direction! That can occur, for example, if a closing quote immediately follows a dash, or if an apostrophe showing contraction appears at the *start* of a word. ('Tis rare, but it happens.) You can fix it by deleting the old quote and inserting an extra space or letter for just long enough to get a new quote curled the right way.

Word may also curl the quote the wrong way if you have improperly inserted a space between the enclosed text and a closing quote. For example, if a sentence ends in a period, there should be no space between the period and a closing quote. To quickly find such instances for fixing, search for the combination of a space and a *straight* quote followed by either another space or a paragraph mark.

Also be aware that not *all* quotes should be curled. For instance, a double quote used in place of an inch mark must be straight. So must all quotes within HTML tags or other code snippets shown as samples in your text. If quotes in an HTML tag are curled, the code is invalid!

To get *straight* quotes, just turn off "smart quotes" in AutoFormat As You Type long enough to insert them, then restore the setting. Or turn them off and run a Find and Replace, again with straight quotes in both boxes. Or you can copy and paste the straight quotes from elsewhere.

•

Next in importance in book punctuation is to use a true dash, or *em dash*, instead of substituting a single or double hyphen. (It's called an *em dash* because it's about as wide as a capital *M*.) You can insert one manually from the Symbol dialog box or with a special key combination—Alt-Control-Minus on the Windows numeric keypad, Shift-Option-

Hyphen or Command-Option-Minus on the Mac. Note that, in books, the em dash has *no* space before or after.

If you want to be picky about hyphens and dashes, there's another kind of dash that falls between—the *en dash*. This is used to convey a range, as in "2001–2013" or "pages 48–57" or "May–December." It can also connect two terms like a hyphen when one term is *already* hyphenated. This dash too you can insert from the Symbol dialog box or with a special key combination—in this case, Control-Minus on the Windows numeric keypad, Option-Hyphen or Command-Minus on the Mac. And this dash too has *no* spaces around it.

AutoFormat As You Type offers to help with dashes, but this seems less reliable than inserting them manually. If you want to try it, the setting in Word for Windows makes Word replace two hyphens with an em dash. On the Mac, though, the equivalent setting makes Word *also* replace a single hyphen with an en dash. This leaves no easy way to insert a regular hyphen!

●

Oddly, there's one special character available on your computer that looks *worse* than the typewriter equivalent. That's the *ellipsis* (. . .), which marks an omission in text, or a pause in dialog.

The computer version always looks like three periods typed together (...), as they would be on a typewriter. But that works well on a typewriter only because of its monospace font, which spreads them out. For the same effect in the proportional font of a book, the periods must be separated by spaces (. . .). So, that's how you should enter it—as three separate periods with spaces between, as well as before and after.

Of course, the best kind of space to place between the periods is the Nonbreaking Space. That will keep all three on the same line. And if you like, you can use another Nonbreaking Space in front, to keep the ellipsis with the word that comes before it. (I talk more about the Nonbreaking Space in my section on line breaking.)

●

There are many other special characters used in book typography, and one way or another, you can insert nearly all of them in a Word document. For example, from the Special Characters tab of Word's Symbol dialog box, you can insert several legal symbols—for "copyright" (©), "registered" (®), or "trademark" (™).

Moving beyond Word's Symbol command, you can locate and insert symbols on Windows with the Character Map utility. On the Start Menu, choose All Programs > Accessories > System Tools. The advantage here is that you can search on the character name.

On the Mac, there's the Character Viewer. In System Preferences for OS X 10.8 or earlier, choose Language & Text > Input Sources, then turn on "Keyboard & Character Viewer" and "Show Input menu in menu bar;" for OS X 10.9, it's in the Keyboard pane. You can then choose "Show Character Viewer" from the menu.

The problem is that not all the available characters are supported by the Kindle. Ones that aren't may appear on there as strings of jumbled characters or as boxed question marks or may cause more obscure problems, such as font switching.

How do you know which characters will work and which to avoid? Unfortunately, Amazon's documentation of this is spotty, contradictory, and in some cases just plain wrong.

For instance, you can still read on an Amazon KDP Help page that the Kindle supports only the Latin-1 character set, with certain exceptions. Actually, what the Kindle supports is Windows-1252, a successor of Latin-1. More importantly, all Kindles also support UTF-8, a flavor of Unicode, which allows many more characters than Windows-1252 (including the "exceptions" that Amazon wrongly says can't be used). What's more, the current Amazon software for creating Kindle books takes any other encoding, including Windows-1252, and *converts* it to UTF-8.

The Unicode character set, though, is much too large for common fonts to encompass, so Kindle fonts support only a portion of it—and that portion varies. Generally, the newer Kindles will display more characters—but there are reportedly also characters on the older Kindles that some newer ones won't show!

In light of the uncertainties, I suggest limiting yourself to the most basic characters that will work for you—including the ones I've discussed here. If less common characters are essential, you can still try them, but test as widely as you can and keep an eye out for customer complaints.

Of course, one case in which special characters are essential is when you're publishing in a language that requires them. Here's a list of languages that the Kindle currently supports.

kdp.amazon.com/help?topicId=A9FDO0A3V0119

•

Among the special characters you can insert in Word and export to HTML are several just to control formatting features like spacing, hyphenation, and line breaking. These are most easily found on the Special Characters tab of the Symbol dialog.

I'll discuss the use of some of these later, but for now, it's important to understand that most are *not* supported on Kindle. Amazon advises you to avoid any special spaces and formatting characters other than the nonbreaking space and the zero width non-joiner—which Word calls the No-Width Optional Break (offered on Windows only).

One problem character is Word's Optional Hyphen— called *soft hyphen* in HTML—which is meant to be visible only when a word is split between two lines. This character works fine on some Kindles but on others will show as a regular hyphen even in the *middle* of a line. Any Optional Hyphens, then, should just be removed, using the Special menu of Word's Find and Replace. Note that, in some cases, you may find these hyphens in your document even if you didn't insert them yourself. For example, if your text was scanned, Optional Hyphens may have been added during OCR.

Though you can use nonbreaking spaces safely, there are a couple of caveats. First, Amazon asks you not to string them together to form extended spaces, as is sometimes done in HTML. Second, unlike in Word, nonbreaking spaces on Kindle won't keep a fixed width in justified text. Instead, they'll expand like normal spaces.

Font Formatting

On the Kindle, font choice is offered mostly for the sake of the Kindle user, not the publisher. The publisher's control of fonts is spotty at best. On some Kindles, you can't control them at all, and on others, you may wind up with a font entirely different from what you expect.

On most newer Kindles, the default font is Georgia, and it's a good choice for digital text—strong and highly readable. So, I suggest you make this the primary font in your Word document and just leave it at that. (On older Kindles, this choice will be ignored in favor of the default Caecilia.)

One thing about Georgia, though, is that it has old-fashioned numerals, which may not work for technical writing. In that case, you might instead use Arial for all or part of your book. On newer Kindles, that will give you either Arial or Helvetica, while on older Kindles, it will be ignored. (When possible, this book uses Arial to show HTML code, Web addresses, and such.)

Unfortunately, there are no other fonts available across all newer Kindles, other than the primitive Caecilia. So, there's not much point in venturing beyond Georgia and Arial unless you intend to embed a font—which is beyond the scope of this book. (Though Amazon claims that Courier or "monospace" is available across all Kindles—a claim repeated almost everywhere—text specified in either of those ways will display on the Paperwhite as Helvetica.)

You can experiment with other fonts, though, if you don't mind them showing up only on *some* Kindles. On the Kindle Fire, for example, you can choose among Arial, Caecilia,

Courier, Georgia, Lucida, Times New Roman, Trebuchet, and Verdana. On the Paperwhite, there's Baskerville, Caecilia, Caecilia Condensed, Futura, Helvetica, and Palatino. And the desktop Kindles will display any font on the host computer. Of course, to specify a font in Word, you'll need that font on your own computer.

If you're trying different fonts, don't be fooled by the Kindle Fire emulation in the desktop Kindle Previewer. This emulation will display any font you select in Word—but only because it's on your computer! You won't have that range on the actual device.

●

Some Kindle models will show any font size accurately, but others are limited to common sizes, with the sizes in between shifted higher or lower. At the same time, you want to mostly avoid using extreme sizes, because the Kindle needs headroom to adjust size in accord with user settings. The best idea, then, is to stick mostly to point sizes 10, 12, 14, and 18, with 12 for basic text and with a possible stretch to 24 points in a pinch.

On older Kindles, though, the difference in font sizes is "compressed." So, for example, what is displayed for 24-point text is not nearly twice as large as what's shown for 12-point type. You can't do anything about that, but you'll want to be aware of it.

●

To emphasize words in basic text, the convention for books is to style them with italics instead of bolding or underlining. Bolding, of course, is fine for headings or other isolated text. Underlining seldom has any place in a book other than to denote links or to emulate typewritten text.

Superscripts and subscripts work just fine in Kindle books. Just apply them normally in Word. But as in Word, you may have to impose an exact line spacing to prevent them from forcing lines farther apart. (I'll talk about line spacing later.)

Small caps work on newer Kindles and are just ignored on older ones. So, for readers who will see them, they can provide a nice touch to chapter beginnings in literary works.

•

Make sure your font color is set to Automatic—not black! This enables the Kindle to change the text color to white when the user goes into Night mode, as allowed on some Kindles. If your font color is instead set to black, the text will *disappear* against the black background of that mode, and you'll get complaints that your book is full of blank pages!

Even if you've set the color correctly, it's a good idea to check for stray black text before you export to HTML. It's too easy to paste in such text from another document and not be aware of the difference. Search by using the Format menu in the Find and Replace dialog box, with your cursor placed in the Find box but without entering text.

•

Word will apply the Hyperlink and FollowedHyperlink character styles to any internal or external links you add for navigation—including, for example, links in a table of contents. These styles may be set up with a different font than you expect, so it's a good idea to check that. (Depending on your Styles dialog settings, one or both styles may not appear if you haven't already inserted a hyperlink and followed it. In that case, set the dialog options to show "All Styles.")

At the same time, you can choose different link colors. Just keep in mind that the text must show up well and look good in all modes—Normal, Sepia, and Night.

Paragraph Styles

As when designing any kind of book with Word, you should use the Styles feature to keep your paragraph formatting consistent and give you greater control. When Word exports to HTML, your paragraph styles become a key feature in the HTML document, so their proper use is essential.

Get used to working in the Styles dialog box, accessible from the icon at the lower right of the Styles command group on the Ribbon. That's where the real power of Word's styles is available. Also, as I recommended earlier, be sure you've turned off the Editing option "Keep track of formatting" to prevent a proliferation of styles!

If you're on a Mac, watch out for one little gotcha when creating, modifying, or deleting styles: Word will not save a document if those are the only changes you've made. You must also have changed something in the document's content—even if it's only adding a space and then deleting it.

•

By default, Word will apply the Normal style to your paragraphs. Amazon knows this, so for some Kindles, it *hijacks* that style, changing its formatting to what Amazon prefers. This can lead, for example, to unwanted space above or below a paragraph.

If you want control of your own formatting, then, you'll have to avoid the Normal style and apply something different. There's no problem, though, with applying styles *based on* Normal, or even with applying a duplicate of Normal under a different name.

In regard to this, watch out for manual page breaks in recent versions of Word. Unless you're in Compatibility Mode, each break is now placed in a paragraph of its own, and the Normal style is assigned automatically. That in itself isn't a problem—but if you then hit Return and start typing, your new paragraph will be in Normal as well. (This is another reason to stick to the paragraph format setting "Page break before" to start a new page.)

You can change all paragraphs already in Normal style to a different one by using the Format menu in the Find and Replace dialog. Don't enter any text, but place your cursor in first the Find box and then the Replace while choosing a style for each.

●

Kindles also tend to hijack the formatting of standard heading styles, like Word's Heading 1, Heading 2, and so on. Here again, you can simply assign duplicate styles with different names. Just make sure the names are *really* different. I tried "Head 1" as a style name, and the Kindle converter was smart enough to figure out I was trying to fool it!

The only problem with this evasion is that using standard heading styles can make it easier to set up navigation within the document—for example, to automatically generate a table of contents in Word for Windows. So, you may have to choose what's most important to you.

●

IMPORTANT: With Amazon's move from the old Mobipocket format to Kindle Format 8, some of my paragraph style and formatting tricks may no longer work as reliably on older Kindles. That's because Mobipocket files are now generated in a new way, giving you less control than before.

There's not much you can do about that in Word besides wait for old hardware to die and laggard software to be updated. Over time, your Kindle books will appear correctly to more people.

Paragraph Spacing

For basic text, there are two primary ways to separate paragraphs from one another. On the Web, the convention is to put vertical space between them—a "blank line"—to form *block paragraphs*. But in book typography, the convention is to indent the first line of each paragraph, for *indented paragraphs*. Either of these ways is acceptable in an ebook, though I strongly recommend the first-line indent.

Unfortunately, Microsoft Word has popularized a third way: putting space between *and* indenting the first line. In other words, separating in two ways instead of one. This is redundant, wasteful, and just plain silly. And since most readers seem to ignore this part of my advice, I'll go a little farther and tell you what I *really* think: *It's an abomination.*

Familiarity with Word has seduced most people into considering this third way appropriate. But please understand that in a book, no matter how "right" it may look to you, this is a sign of an amateur. If you want your book to seem professional or anywhere near it, do *not* apply both a first-line indent and space between!

Of course, not all paragraphs will get first-line indents, even if you do choose that as your basic format. Here are some kinds of paragraphs that shouldn't get that indent. (Some might instead need space between.)

• A paragraph preceded by empty space anyway, as at the beginning of a chapter or other text division. (In this case, the indent would be redundant.)

• The first (or only) paragraph of a block quote.

• Some of the book's front and back matter.

• A heading.
• A paragraph containing a graphic.

•

You will need to specify a first-line indent for your paragraph, whether or not you want indenting. If you don't specify, older Kindles will indent anyway by a default amount!

Set the first-line indent in Word's Paragraph Format or on the Ruler—preferably in defining a style. (Here we're using *paragraph* in a word-processing sense, meaning any text followed by a Return. In this sense, *all* text is contained in paragraphs, including headings.) For a normal paragraph, a first-line indent of .25 inch or .5 cm is fine.

Unfortunately, if you want *no* first-line indent, you can't just set that. Any Kindle perfectly understands an instruction for zero indent—but because zero first-line indent is the default for both Word and the Web, Word does not bother including this instruction in the HTML it exports. And without the instruction, an older Kindle will indent!

There are two ways around this within Word. The first is to set the first-line indent to .01 inch or cm. The Kindle will indent the line by that amount—but for the reader, it will be too slight to notice.

The second way is to apply a paragraph style containing a first-line indent, then remove that indent with *direct* paragraph formatting. This forces Word to include *both* instructions in its exported HTML. (This solution might suggest you could instead apply an unindented paragraph style based on an indented one—but that doesn't work.)

If your paragraph is centered, you can ignore the above complication and just specify no indent. No Kindle will try to indent the first line of a centered paragraph unless told to.

●

Space between paragraphs is specified with the Spacing Before and After settings in Word's Paragraph Format. If you're indenting the first line of your paragraph, then both of these spacing settings would normally be zero. If you're not indenting, or if you need space between certain paragraphs anyway, I recommend you set Spacing After to 12 points ("12 pt").

Older Kindles will sometimes ignore a paragraph's Spacing Before, so you should normally stick to Spacing After. Spacing Before is apparently safe, though, if the paragraph is centered or right-aligned.

Just as older Kindles will indent a paragraph's first line when given no instruction, both older and newer Kindles will add space after a paragraph by default. But in this case, there's no need to set minimal spacing to avoid this, because Word conveniently does that for you—not in the document, but in the exported HTML!

●

At least some Kindles allow the user to adjust *line spacing*— the distance from the base of one line to the base of the next line higher or lower. So, it's usually best not to try to control this yourself, at least for basic body type. To leave it to the Kindle and the user, simply set your line spacing to "Single."

There are times, though, when you might well want to control it—for example, if you have superscripts that would force some lines farther apart, making the spacing irregular. In that case, the best way is through the "Multiple" setting in the Paragraph Format dialog. This defines line spacing in relation to type size, so that the spacing will increase or decrease as the user makes the type larger or smaller.

For instance, a setting of Multiple 1.25 would give you a line spacing that's 125% the type size. If the size was 12 points, the line spacing would be 15 points (about average for a book). Note, though, that Word calculates this multiple in a non-standard way—so, Word will incorrectly display the spacing as larger than it should be and as larger than it *will* be on the Kindle. Also note that Kindles do not accept a line space percentage lower than 120%.

Don't impose a strict line spacing on a paragraph containing a picture, or the picture could disappear! For such paragraphs, line spacing should always be "Single."

Paragraph Justification

In most books, paragraphs of basic text are *justified,* with a smooth right edge created by adding space between words as needed. This is one case, though, where you might want to depart from standard book typography. The reason is that the Kindle's justification is simply awful.

Most Kindles try to justify without hyphenating longer words at the ends of lines. As a result, the spaces between words can vary wildly in size, creating ridiculously uneven text. And Amazon, knowing no better, proudly displays it in its Kindle advertisements! (Kindle for iPhone *does* hyphenate, even in unjustified text, but usually in the wrong places—and even in headings! Unfortunately, there's no way to turn that off.)

Even worse is that Kindles justify chapter titles and other headings that should be flush left. This doesn't affect a heading that fits on one line, but you'll see it in a heading that overflows to a second. The larger font size aggravates the spaces between words, making these headings look truly horrible.

So, you might well want to avoid justification in favor of *left alignment*—a smooth left edge but a ragged right. But that presents us with another tricky situation—just as when we wanted to unindent paragraphs. Word *can* issue an HTML instruction for left alignment but normally *doesn't,* because that's already the default for both Word and HTML. And in this case, there's no incremental measurement to use as a fudge.

That leaves a solution like the *second* one I gave for unindenting: Apply a style that includes text justification, then use direct paragraph formatting to change to left alignment. Again, this forces Word to include the needed code when exporting HTML. Be careful, though. A solution like this has to be used consistently, because you don't want to accidentally mix justified and unjustified body text.

Now, I understand that some readers of this book will decide they *want* their Kindle text justified, because, after all, it just "looks right." (In other words, they've grown used to seeing it look wrong.) But even if that's your choice, there are still elements that may need a forced left alignment—including headings and lines of verse.

Again, such elements aren't justified unless broken into two or more lines—but almost *any* line might be broken when read with a large enough font or on a mobile phone.

•

I have to warn you: If you prevent justification for body text, Amazon may ask you to change it, citing either complaints from customers or a quality review of its own. It may even check up to see if you've complied. Yes, Amazon is so in love with the Kindle's amateurish justification that it tries to enforce it.

Personally, I find the Kindle's justification so horrendous that I've just told Amazon I refuse to allow it. And so far, Amazon has respected that and backed off. But if you see that the text in this book is justified, it means I've capitulated—at least until Amazon looks away and I can upload a new version.

•

Because of Amazon's campaign to hijack your formatting, you can't ensure your text won't *ever* be justified. So, it's best to prepare for the worst by making sure that justification won't completely ruin your formatting.

One thing this means is that you should never use Manual Line Breaks (Shift-Return) to end list items or lines of poetry. If you do, short lines will be stretched from margin to margin as the Kindle justifies them. Instead, compose each line as a separate paragraph ending with a Paragraph Mark (Return). To separate a poem's verses, add Spacing After to the last line of each one.

Again, this is not a problem when a paragraph is centered.

Line Breaking

One advantage of print publishing is that you can look for awkward line breaking—for instance, places where a line ends between two words that should not be separated—and fix them manually. You don't get that opportunity on the Kindle. With size variations in screen, font, and margin, you never know where lines of text will end.

In your role as book designer, you might actually welcome this, seeing it as freeing you from the tyranny of print perfectionism. On the other hand, it may gall you that your Kindle book looks determinedly amateurish, and you may cast about for ways to tilt the scale more toward professionalism.

On the Special Characters tab of the Symbol dialog, Word offers several tools for controlling line breaking. For the Kindle, some will work better and be more useful than others.

●

Your primary tool for controlling Kindle line breaking is Word's Nonbreaking Space. By inserting it between vulnerable words and numbers, you can guarantee they'll stick together *in case* the Kindle tries to tear them apart. Besides finding it on the Special Characters tab, you can insert it from the keyboard with Control-Shift-Space. On the Mac, Option-Space works as well.

Here are some types of phrases you might want to protect with one or more Nonbreaking Spaces. (Enlarge or reduce your font size to see how the example phrases hold together.)

• Names with initials. Examples: J. R. R. Tolkien, B. Good.

    • Names with abbreviated titles. Examples: Mr. Shepard, Ms. Watson, Dr. Doom.

    • Measurements. Examples: 1 inch, 45 days, 72 ppi.

    • Numbered or "lettered" items. Examples: Heading 1, Format 8, OS X.

    • Times and dates. Examples: 7:00 a.m., 12 noon, October 7, May 1974.

As you can see, many of these phrase types include numbers. So, one way to locate prospective phrases for protection is to run a Word search on "Any Digit," selected from the Special menu. For initials, you could search for a sequence made up of a space, "Any Letter," and a period. Even better is to train yourself to watch for such phrases while you're first typing the text and to insert the Nonbreaking Space at that time.

•

Protecting phrases with the Nonbreaking Space can be helpful even when text is headed for print. But for Kindle publishing, perfectionists might want to go further, using this character to avoid other kinds of awkward line breaking. For instance, I don't like seeing the pronoun *I* or the article *a* hanging at the end of a line when they start a sentence or clause—and especially when they follow a dash. I would much rather move the word down to be with what follows.

For a print book, I would simply look for such instances at the text's right margin and insert a line break before the word. But for Kindle, I would have to insert a Nonbreaking Space after every instance that *might* wind up at the end of a line. This would provide protection *in case* it was needed.

For limited cases, I could do this with a simple find-and-replace. One example would be for the *worst* case—when these words follow a dash. For that, I would search for any *I* or *a* preceded by a dash and followed by a space. I would then replace the final space with a Nonbreaking Space, selected from the Special menu.

But if I wanted to provide protection in a wide *variety* of cases, I'd turn to a little-used feature of Word's: what it calls *wildcard searches*. No, I'm not talking about the usual wildcards you see on the Special menu. When you check the "Use wildcards" option in Word's Advanced Find and Replace, that menu changes, and you gain search capabilities not unlike those of a good code editor. (For details, search Word Help for "wildcards.")

With that option checked, the following two operations *together* would keep *I* or *a* away from the end of a line whenever it followed a punctuation mark. The letters in the second pair of brackets from the end are capital *I* and *A* and lower-case *a*. The apparently empty pairs of square brackets each enclose a regular space. Note that I assume the text has *no* double spaces between sentences. The Replace is identical for each operation and simply substitutes a Nonbreaking Space for the final regular one.

I also assume you're using curly quotes—so you may have to change them here if you're not. The first operation includes both single and double *closing* quotes, while the second includes single and double *opening* quotes. (You can enlarge your text to see them more clearly.) If you like, exclude the comma from the first operation to moderate the changes to your text.

Find: ([.\?\!'",;:\)][ ][IAa])[ ]

Replace: \1^s

Find: ([—""\(][IAa])[ ]

Replace: \1^s

Wildcard searches are especially powerful, so you should always first test carefully on a file copy you can afford to lose. Also, if you're able to copy and paste these samples—don't! They include special characters meant only to help them display better. (Besides that, if you try to paste wildcards in Word for the Mac, the program may insert extra characters.)

Let's look at what these do in practice. In the following passage, you should see *no* line breaking after the word *I*. Go ahead and try it at different sizes. (I'm cheating here a little, because, to fit my own workflow, I'm adding nonbreaking spaces in my exported HTML rather than in Word—but the effect is the same.)

I came. I saw. I conquered. I came. I saw.
I conquered. I came. I saw. I conquered. I came,
I saw, I conquered. I came, I saw, I conquered.
I came, I saw, I conquered. I came; I saw;
I conquered. I came; I saw; I conquered. I came;
I saw; I conquered. I came—I saw—I conquered.
I came—I saw—I conquered. I came—I saw—
I conquered. I came! I saw! I conquered! I came!
I saw! I conquered! I came! I saw! I conquered!

Obviously, the wildcard operations above are not the kind of things you want to retype every time you need them. So, it's best to record each as a macro and assign it to a menu command or keyboard shortcut. Better yet, combine the two in a single macro with a little cut-and-paste in Word's macro editor.

•

There's another kind of awkward line breaking you should be aware of. For print, we're taught to avoid letting paragraphs end with a line containing only a short, one-syllable word—sometimes called an *orphan*. Again, in print, I would look for actual violations and insert a line break somewhere before. But on the Kindle, I might instead look for *all* short words at paragraph ends and insert a Nonbreaking Space before each. This would make sure that none would *ever* wind up on a line alone.

What's worse than an orphan at the end of a paragraph? An orphan in a *heading*—and that's what you're more than likely to get when your Kindle book is read on an iPhone or other small-screen device. So, even if you ignore potential orphans at the ends of paragraphs, you'll probably want to make sure that any short words at the ends of your headings get a Nonbreaking Space in front.

Here's a sample heading, first without protection and then with the Nonbreaking Space before the final word. Change the font size on your Kindle if necessary to see the effect.

A Brief Guide to Really Making Out

A Brief Guide to Really Making Out

You can protect against orphans in paragraphs and headings by inserting Nonbreaking Spaces manually, but in *most* cases, you can instead turn to wildcard searching. The following two operations work in current versions of Word for both Windows and Mac, but *not* in Word 2004 for Mac!

Together, they will place a Nonbreaking Space in front of almost any word or number made up of four characters or fewer at the end of a paragraph, heading, list item, or other text element. The apparently empty set of square brackets in front of each has a regular space inside. The Replace is identical for each. For these operations to work, you must *first* remove any spaces before paragraph marks. The first one also assumes you're using curly quotes, and this one includes both single and double *closing* quotes. Again, test carefully!

Find: [ ]([a-zA-Z0-9]{1,4}[.\?\!'":\)]{1,}^13)

Replace: ^s\1

Find: [ ]([a-zA-Z0-9]{1,4}^13)

Replace: ^s\1

You can alter the maximum number of characters in affected words by changing the number *4* to a higher or lower number. More characters will give you fewer orphans but more unevenness in the preceding line.

With these operations too, you'll probably want to record them as macros and possibly merge them with others.

●

For print publishing, another important tool for controlling line breaking is Word's Nonbreaking Hyphen. Phrases in this book alone that could use its protection include "Latin-1," "Windows-1252," "ISO 8859-1," "UTF-8," "12-point," "Option-8," and "6-8." But as I said before, this character works right only on *some* Kindles, while on others it may cause problems that include a change of font for the entire book.

The loss of this tool is a nuisance, to say the least. If you're able to work in HTML, there are effective workarounds—at least for newer Kindles, which are now the majority—and I discuss them in my book *HTML Fixes for Kindle*. But even in Word, you can jury-rig a replacement.

This solution relies on two dirty little secrets. The first is that newer Kindles will not break a line on either side of an HTML tag, such as is used for formatting.

So, let's say we take the phrase "UTF-8" and make the hyphen italic—*just* the hyphen, mind you. Or if the phrase currently has a Nonbreaking Hyphen, let's say we *replace* that with a regular hyphen in italic. Either way, you can do it quickly throughout the document with Word's Find-and-Replace and its Formatting and Special menus.

Now, when Word exports to HTML, those regular hyphens will be enclosed by italics tags, like this:

```
UTF<i>-</i>8
```

Newer Kindles will then keep the entire phrase on the same line. So, in effect, we have a nonbreaking hyphen!

The *second* dirty little secret is what lets us get away with exploiting the first one. There is no italic hyphen! Or rather, italic hyphens are identical to regular ones. So, making those hyphens italic doesn't really change your text.

What if the entire phrase is already italic? No problem. Just replace the italic hyphen with a regular one, again using the Format menu of Find and Replace. Here's what is then exported:

```
<i>UTF</i>-<i>8</i>
```

The hyphen is still surrounded by tags, so this too would be protected from line breaking.

Note that these tricks have the *reverse* effect on *older* Kindles, allowing breaks where the Kindle wouldn't otherwise make them. But at this point, it's more important to get it right on newer Kindles.

●

Still another good tool in Word—sadly, on Windows only, while missing in Word for Mac—is the No-Width Optional Break. There's no keyboard shortcut for this one, so it must be inserted from the Special Characters tab. When exported to HTML, it becomes the *zero width non-joiner*.

This character is something like an Optional Hyphen without the hyphen. You can use it to indicate preferred break points for Web addresses, code, and other long strings of characters that are likely to be divided between lines but should *not* be hyphenated. Without this, the Kindle may break the line randomly, wherever it runs out of room.

To see how it works, look at the following Web address. As you can see, without an Optional Break, it tends to break confusingly. On older Kindles, an unwanted hyphen may be inserted at the break, or text may actually disappear past the right margin. (If it's all fitting on one line on your Kindle, increase the font size until it runs over.)

www.aaronshep.com/kidwriter/books/Business.html

Now here it is again *with* an Optional Break after each slash.

www.aaronshep.com/kidwriter/books/Business.html

OK, since I'm on a Mac, I had to cheat a little: I inserted a substitute code that I replaced later, while automatically processing the book's HTML. (I could have inserted a zero width non-joiner in Word with OS X's Character Viewer, but Word would not have exported it properly anyway.) If your Web address is hyperlinked, replacing a substitute code might be more convenient in Word for Windows as well, since Word's Hyperlink dialogs are not friendly to formatting characters. (For details, see *HTML Fixes for Kindle*.)

The No-Width Optional Break is extremely useful when it works—but in text for Kindle, that isn't as often as you might like. In fact, I've given up trying to figure out all the positions in which it does or does not work properly. The list varies on different Kindles, and sometimes on the *same* Kindle. Pinning it down is complicated by the fact that, even without the Optional Break, different Kindles break lines in different places.

My general advice, then, is to insert the Optional Break wherever you think it might be helpful, then hope for the best. But there are a couple of caveats, too. Most importantly, the Optional Break is best used in left-aligned text. That's because some older Kindles treat it more like a thin space, allowing text on either side to move apart when justified.

Also, you must take care never to place the Optional Break right after a point where character formatting changes—for instance, from regular to italics or back again, or from one font to another. On older e-ink Kindles, this can cause a repeat of text from *before* that point!

●

Whenever you shift any text from one line to the next, there's a price to pay. In left-aligned text, it will make your lines less even. In justified text, it will increase spacing between words—and with the absence of hyphenation on the Kindle, this can get to the point of looking really bad.

In print, you can often find a way to even things out within the paragraph, but that's obviously not possible on the Kindle. So, when deciding how much to adjust, you'll need to find a good balance, weighing the cost of your changes against the benefit.

Of course, this is also another argument for avoiding justified text on the Kindle!

Page Layout

You may be used to creating vertical space in text by hitting Return repeatedly to insert new, blank paragraphs. If so, you'll have to forget that, as not all Kindles will display the space. But there are two good alternatives.

The first is to add large amounts of Spacing Before or After in Word's paragraph formatting. I recommend that you stick mostly to Spacing After, because, as I said earlier, Spacing Before does not always work on some Kindles. But Spacing Before does seem safe when applied to paragraphs that are centered or right-aligned. (It can also work in a paragraph that follows a page break, but there's a complication I'll discuss shortly.)

The second way is to add any number of blank lines to the beginning of a paragraph by hitting *Shift*-Return, giving you a Manual Line Break instead of a Paragraph Mark. (You can easily see the difference on screen if you've told Word to display invisible characters.) For some reason, the Kindle prefers the line break. But don't add the lines at the *end* of the paragraph. If that paragraph is justified—through your intention or the Kindle's insistence—a short last line of text will be spread across the page.

Again, there should be *no* extra space in continuous text between paragraphs that have first-line indents.

●

Unfortunately, some newer Kindles do not respect any space between a page break and the following content. In other words, after a page break—whether manual or automatic—

content is always placed against the top edge of the reading area. Yuck.

The reason for this relates to Kindle Format 8, the updated Kindle format that was introduced with the Kindle Fire. KF8 is based loosely on its competitor ebook format EPUB, and in that format, you normally produce page breaks by splitting your text among multiple files. KF8 *does* also honor page breaks *within* a text file, but Amazon has never bothered to make them work flawlessly.

To completely fix this problem, you'd probably have to give up working in Word entirely and move to an ebook editor that outputs a Kindle book as multiple text files before packaging them. Short of that, the only solution is to place *some* kind of extra content right after your page break.

I used to recommend doing this by inserting a more-or-less innocuous punctuation mark in a centered paragraph at page top. But I've now replaced that with a transparent GIF, which is normally invisible on all Kindles in all modes. (I've used that in this book on the pages with numbered chapter headings, among others.)

You can create a transparent GIF in a program like Photoshop (as explained in *Pictures on Kindle*), but you can also produce one in Word. Here's the procedure:

1. Insert a rectangle or any other shape in a paragraph at the top of the page.

2. Change the wrapping style to "In Line with Text."

3. Adjust the size and shape as convenient. If you like, you can make it as tall as the space you want empty; or you can make it short and later apply Spacing After to the paragraph.

4. Remove the border by choosing "No Outline" or "No Line."

5. Set the fill to 100% transparency. (To reach this setting, you may have to choose "More Fill Colors" or call up the Format Shape dialog box.) Do *not* choose "No Fill"!

When exporting the document to HTML, Word will convert this transparent shape to a GIF. As with other pictures, you'll have to bundle the GIF with your HTML file when submitting, as explained later.

In the spirit of full disclosure: Until it has "warmed up," a non-backlit e-ink Kindle may display a little "dirt" along some part of the edge of a transparent GIF, rendering it not perfectly invisible. Rather than give up my transparent GIFs, I've chosen to pretend that the Kindle always works as intended.

●

While newer Kindles may ignore any space you want at the top of a page, older Kindles may add a little space you *don't* want—if the page in your Word document was started with a manual page break or section break. So, as I suggested earlier, it's better to start a new page by formatting the first paragraph with "Page break before."

If your page is headed by a transparent GIF or any other content you've inserted just for spacing, apply "Page break before" to the paragraph with that content—*not* to the heading or other text that follows.

●

At this writing, all Kindles ignore formatting instructions to "Keep with next" or "Keep lines together." (And Word for the Mac doesn't include such instructions in its HTML anyway.) So, forget about trying to avoid page breaks in awkward places. That includes having single lines of text that are stranded at the top or bottom of a page—called *widows* and *orphans*, in another use of that term.

After all, this is the Kindle. Typographic niceties need not apply.

3
Special Elements

Other Paragraphs

Block quotes are normally created by indenting the paragraph as a whole and adding space before and after. But since Spacing Before does not always work for the Kindle, instead add Spacing After to both the block quote and the paragraph above it. Here's a sample:

> For your block quote, don't forget to set a minimal first-line indent of .01 inch or cm in Word to keep the Kindle from displaying a larger one.

Though any Kindle will honor a whole-paragraph left indent, a *right* indent will work only on newer Kindles. But that may be just as well. Since the line of type on some Kindles is already so short, it's probably best in any case to indent only on the left.

Kindles are wildly inconsistent in how they scale indents in relation to font size—both among different Kindles and sometimes even among different types of indent. This can throw off the positioning of your block quotes, making them look odd. Sadly, there's nothing you can do about it, short of avoiding block quotes.

•

A *hanging indent*—another kind of indent specified on Word's Ruler or in the Paragraph Format dialog box—leaves a paragraph's first line as is but indents the lines that come after. This format is often used, for example, for items in a bibliography or for speeches in a script. It's also used for poetry. Each line of verse is made a separate paragraph, so that the overrun from long lines will be indented.

The problem is that older Kindles and newer Kindles require different HTML code to make this happen. What works for newer Kindles simply makes older ones indent all lines equally—by different amounts on different Kindles. What works for older Kindles makes newer ones shove the beginnings of first lines into the left margin, where on some Kindles (but not all), they disappear.

Among Kindle experts, the standard solution is to modify the book's HTML so that different Kindles read different code. But this is beyond the technical abilities of most self publishers. Besides that, it may run afoul of Amazon itself trying to fix the problem.

Given the mess that Amazon has created, I feel that the best approach is to avoid hanging indents whenever possible. Most of the time, you can convert to block paragraphs—space between, no first-line indent (or rather, a minimal one, to prevent some Kindles from indenting more). This will certainly work for bibliographies and scripts. After all, the main purpose of the hanging indent is to eliminate the spaces needed between block paragraphs—and that economy is a benefit more with printed books than with ebooks.

Of course, standard block paragraphs won't work for individual lines of poetry, but you might try a variant. Each line of verse in the following sample is a block paragraph with line spacing set to Multiple 1.2—the minimum accepted by Kindle—but also with a subtle Spacing After of just 3 points. So, if a single line of verse—in other words, a single paragraph—overflows to a second displayed line, the distance between the two will be slightly less than their distance to other verse lines. The difference is not enough to be awkward but should be enough to register on the reader. On the other hand, the set line spacing of the verse may look strange if it doesn't match surrounding text. (Enlarge the type on your Kindle if none of the following lines run over.)

What a to-do to die today at a minute or two to two,

a thing distinctly hard to say but harder still to do.

for they'll beat a tattoo at a quarter to two, a rat-ta-tat tat-ta-tat tat-ta-tat-to.

and the dragon will come when he hears the drum,

at a minute or two to two today, at a minute or two to two.

A similar approach could work for multiple lines of sample HTML or other code, for which a hanging indent usually isn't even wanted. (Again, enlarge the type on your Kindle if no lines run over.)

```
<meta name=Title content="From Word to Kindle">
<meta http-equiv=Content-Type content="text/html;
charset=utf-8">
<meta name=ProgId content=Word.Document>
<meta name=Generator content="Microsoft Word 11">
<meta name=Originator content="Microsoft Word 11">
<title>From Word to Kindle</title>
```

The truth is, though, that nothing really takes the place of hanging indents in poetry—and for that reason, I use them myself, despite the problems. And Word's exported code for hanging indents works fine on newer Kindles. On older ones, you lose the hanging indent and get odd whole-paragraph indenting—but it never looks *too* terrible, as long as the hanging indent you've set is modest.

As an example, each of the following verse lines has a hanging indent of .17 inch. (In other words, approximately 1 em for 12-point type—an *em* being a common typographer's unit of measure.)

What a to-do to die today at a minute or two to two,
a thing distinctly hard to say but harder still to do.
for they'll beat a tattoo at a quarter to two, a rat-ta-tat tat-ta-
     tat tat-ta-tat-to.
and the dragon will come when he hears the drum,
at a minute or two to two today, at a minute or two to two.

It's also possible to *combine* the hanging indent and my line spacing trick, in that way providing visual cues on both new and old Kindles. Here's a sample:

What a to-do to die today at a minute or two to two,

a thing distinctly hard to say but harder still to do.

for they'll beat a tattoo at a quarter to two, a rat-ta-tat tat-ta-
     tat tat-ta-tat-to.

and the dragon will come when he hears the drum,

at a minute or two to two today, at a minute or two to two.

Lists

People spend far too much time struggling to make Word's automatic lists work as they want. There is no trick at all to making a list in Word and exporting it for Kindle. Let me show you with these two examples.

- Item 1
- Item 2
- Item 3

1. Item 1
2. Item 2
3. Item 3

Neither of these lists was created with Word's automatic list commands. You absolutely don't need them. In fact, I have not used them once since discovering it was simpler to create lists by hand.

If you're puzzling about how to create the bullet points, you can add one from Word's Symbol dialog box, then copy it and paste it to anywhere else you need it. Or, on the Mac, just press Option-8. And instead of following the bullet or number with a tab, which doesn't work on the Kindle, use a space. (For justified text in *print*, you might use a Nonbreaking Space to keep the space from being expanded—but the Kindle expands it anyway.)

True, this does make you lose out on automatic HTML lists when you export. But again, you don't really need them. Sometimes it's just easier to do it yourself.

•

If you do use Word's automatic lists, it's a good idea to go into the dialog box for this function and change the bullet or numbers font to match the font of your main text. Note that these fonts for automatic elements cannot be found with Word's Find command, because they're not really in the text itself!

Tables

Yes, you can create a table in Word and have it exported in your HTML. But such tables work well only on newer Kindles—and on the oldest, they don't work at all. (Also note that hyperlinks never work in Kindle tables.)

If you can present your info in a straight vertical format, it's best to do that instead. Another approach is to use a table but to design it so the text still appears in a logical order if an old Kindle flattens it to a single column.

Amazon's own recommendation is to present your table as a graphic—preferably a GIF—which will display on all Kindles. Getting this to look good is not as easy as you might think, but tips for it are in my book *Pictures on Kindle*. Here's a sample of what you can produce.

Key	Length	I.D.
G	16"	11/16" +
F	18"	3/4" +
E	19"	13/16" +
D	21"	7/8" +
C	23"	15/16" +

Text Boxes and Sidebars

Using Word's Borders and Shading dialog box, it's possible to create boxes around paragraphs and even to shade the insides, all in a way that will carry over to your exported HTML. But some older Kindles won't display the shading, and some won't display the border either—and even those that normally show one or both may sometimes fail at it, if the box contains more than one paragraph. So, I don't recommend including boxes in your design.

●

Without reliable boxes, it's impossible to produce a proper sidebar that will display correctly on all Kindles. But you can at least give the impression of one, as shown on the following page.

SAMPLE SIDEBAR

This sidebar is set apart by top and bottom borders created in Photoshop and imported into Word. As you can see, the borders are "directional"—meaning they have elements that make them seem to point inward toward the text. This allows them to work even if the sidebar text extends beyond a single page.

In this case, I achieved the sense of direction by including three shades of gray, arranged with lighter shades toward the inside. (Note that none of the shades are pure black, which would disappear in Night mode.) I could have done the same with sets of lines of different thicknesses, or rows of triangles pointing up or down, or . . . Well, I'll let you come up with variations of your own. We don't want all Kindle books to look alike!

I've further enhanced the separation by setting the text in Arial instead of my usual Georgia—though I know that won't show on all Kindles.

To make the sidebar start on a new page, I applied the paragraph format setting "Page break before" to the paragraph containing the top border. If I had instead inserted a manual page break, some Kindles would push the border a little way down the page—not good layout for a sidebar!

Footnotes and Endnotes

Standard footnotes and endnotes in Word automatically export to HTML as endnotes. Word will also automatically place links both ways between each note and its reference marker in the main text. (I'll talk more about such internal links later.) So, it's possible to handle notes in your document just as you're used to—but this is a clunky arrangement at best.

One alternative is to place each note immediately following the paragraph it refers to. You can separate it from the main text with horizontal lines above and below, inserted from the Borders menu or Borders and Shading dialog box.* Be sure to click "Horizontal Line" instead of adding an actual border! These inserted lines are graphics that are replaced with code when Word exports to HTML.

---

* Here's an example.

But that too is awkward. Better would probably be to merge notes with the main text—either within the referring paragraph or forming another paragraph just below—and to set it off with parentheses. (Like so.)

Or perhaps best yet, consider whether anything relegated to such notes is really important enough to call for interrupting the flow of your ebook. You might then decide to relegate notes to a print edition, which would better accommodate subsidiary text.

Pictures

Picture editing is a huge topic in itself, and I cover it in a separate book, *Pictures on Kindle*. But here are a few tips on pictures as they relate specifically to Word.

First off, let's be clear that picture handling is *not* one of Word's strong points. In fact, Word may well be the worst possible choice for a Kindle book in which pictures are important. The program seems to claim an unlimited license to tamper with your pictures, and how it does that can vary wildly from one Word version to the next.

Still, in a document meant for export to HTML, it's possible to handle your pictures in such a way that Word simply lets them pass through with little or no change. The following tips should ensure this, as well as make sure the picture is properly positioned in your Kindle book.

•

In your version of Word, locate the Web Options and make sure the following is *deselected*: "Allow PNG as an output format." (Oddly, the Web Options setting for picture resolution has no effect.)

Add only JPEGs and GIFs. Any other format will be converted to one of these anyway, but you won't be able to control how Word does it.

JPEGs must be 72 ppi for Mac or 96 ppi for Windows. A GIF, on the other hand, is by definition *always* 72 ppi—but Word for Windows treats it as 96 ppi anyway. (The *ppi* stands for "pixels per inch," a measure of image resolution. You'll sometimes instead see *dpi*—"dots per inch"—but that's actually a measure of *printer* resolution, not image.)

For both JPEG and GIF, stay within Word's maximum picture size of 22 inches (55+ cm) on a side. At 96 ppi for Windows, that's 2112 pixels. At 72 ppi for the Mac, it's 1584.

•

To add a picture, use Word's command to insert it from the file. *Do not* drag or paste it in. For safety and convenience, make sure the insert dialog is set to actually insert the picture rather than "Link to File."

To *repeat* a picture, you should copy and paste within the document instead of inserting again. With this method, Word may output the picture only once, with multiple links to it—though Word's behavior in this is inconsistent from one version to another.

Place the picture in a blank paragraph with "Single" line spacing, centered, with no indent for either the first line or the whole paragraph.

Make sure the image is "in line with text"—Word's default—rather than "floating." That means you must ignore Word's options to let text "wrap" around the sides of your picture or appear in front or behind it.

•

If Word shrinks the picture to fit within your document's margins, the picture will be exported with reduced pixel dimensions. Specifically, the new pixel dimensions will be the new linear dimensions at 72 ppi for the Mac, or 96 ppi for Windows. In addition, if that shrunk picture is a GIF, some versions of Word will *convert it to JPEG*.

To prevent that resizing and format conversion on export, call up the dialog box that controls the picture's size. Where you find it will depend on your version of Word, and there will be more than one way to reach it. In Word 2010 for

Windows, you can click or double-click on the picture to bring up the Picture Tools, then click the bottom-right icon on the Size command group. On the Mac, you can select the picture and then access the dialog box from the Format menu. On either Windows or Mac, you may also find it by right-clicking or Option-clicking on the picture.

Now *uncheck* "Lock aspect ratio," then click "Reset." Both of the scaling dimensions should now show at 100%. If the dialog box in your Word version lacks a Reset button, type in these scaling dimensions directly.

When you click "OK" and return to the document, you'll see the picture appropriately enlarged and extending past the right margin—awkward but manageable. What's more important is that Word will now export it at its original pixel dimensions.

The procedure I've described is needed when working in any view for print documents—views called Print Layout and Draft in recent Word versions and Page Layout and Normal in older ones. (Pictures are invisible, though, in Draft View for .docx files.)

As an alternative, in recent Word versions, you can switch to Web Layout. In this view, pictures are inserted at 100% size, and they stay that way when you switch back to other views. (An earlier version of this view, Online Layout, did not work this way.) In fact, Web Layout is not a bad view for editing Kindle books, especially with pictures—except it will not show your added page breaks.

A couple more notes on sizing: Do *not* apply a border to your picture in Word—a border of any width will change the scaling and trigger resizing. Also, if Word displays your

JPEG as smoothed and fuzzy, this does *not* mean the picture itself has been touched.

•

Though a GIF with transparency is best created in your photo editor, you may find it simpler to add transparency to a picture in Word itself—for instance, to a TIFF at the preferred 72 ppi for Mac or 96 ppi for Windows. With transparency added, Word will output the picture as a GIF, regardless of original format.

How the transparency command is accessed will vary among Word versions, but in newer ones, click or double-click the picture to call up the Picture Tools. Then select Recolor > Set Transparent Color, and click on white in the picture, or on any other color you want transparent. For the procedure in older versions, search Word Help for "transparency."

•

If a picture is meant to fill all or most of a page, do *not* add a manual page break or section break before it. In some cases, this can cause the Kindle to display an entire blank page before the picture! Instead, you can apply the setting "Page break before" to the containing paragraph.

•

When exporting, Word by default places your pictures in a separate folder with an associated name. Links to the picture files are included in Word's HTML file, along with the pictures' pixel dimensions. Check the picture files to make sure they came out as expected!

As an alternative to keeping Word from tampering with your pictures, you could replace Word's outputted picture files with your own versions. For more than a few pictures, though, this may be tricky, because Word *renames* them— with names like "image001.jpg," "image002.jpg," and so on, based on their order of appearance. Any time you add, remove, or move a picture within your ebook, this also changes the output filenames of pictures placed after that one.

•

If you don't want to deal with all the complexities of Word picture handling and Kindle flowing text, you can create a *fixed-format* Kindle book, with every element set in position on the page. This works especially well for books dominated by pictures, such as children's picture books.

To create a fixed-format Kindle book from a Word document, export it as PDF instead of HTML, then import it into Amazon's Kindle Comic Creator. You can find it here:

www.amazon.com/kindlepublishing *or*

www.amazon.com/kindleformat

This approach has both advantages and disadvantages. For a full discussion and sample workflow, see *Pictures on Kindle*.

4
Navigation

Web Links

It's easy to link to locations on the Web from within your Word document, and those links will carry through to your Kindle book. Just select the text you want to link and then Insert Hyperlinks. On the "Web Page" tab of the dialog that comes up, place the Web address in the "Link to" field, making sure it starts with the prefix "http://"—or at least with "www" (which should trigger Word to add the other).

Just to remind you, it's usually best to copy and paste Web addresses from your browser's address field rather than risk errors in typing. Also, after creating the link, you should always click it to make sure it works. (In some old versions of Word, you have to Control-click instead.) It may take a few seconds, but Word should then open the link in your browser.

Word may also create links *automatically* for Web addresses placed directly in your text. This is controlled by the "Internet and network paths" option in your "AutoFormat as You Type" settings—an option I personally make sure is turned off.

To edit either the linked text or the Web address for an existing hyperlink, right-click or Control-click it and choose Hyperlink > Edit Hyperlink. In the dialog, you can also click "Remove Link" to return the text to normal.

●

Chances are, you'll want links in your Kindle book to one or more books on Amazon. Don't be confused by the super-long addresses your browser shows you when you visit Amazon's site. Most of this is just Amazon talking to itself about marketing data, plus optimizing the address for Google search.

What you actually need for your link is much shorter. Here's how it looks for this ebook:

http://www.amazon.com/dp/B005FG163Y

For your own book, just replace the ending letter-numeral combination with your own book's ASIN—Amazon Standard Identification Number. You can find that on your book's Amazon page or at Amazon KDP.

For more on Amazon links—including ones with your Amazon Associates ID—see my book *Aiming at Amazon,* or else my Web article "Linking to Amazon" at

www.newselfpublishing.com/AmazonLinking.html

Internal Links

Just as you can link to locations on the Web, you can link to locations within your book. For instance, if you refer your reader to another chapter, you can link to it directly.

Creating such a link is simplest if your destination text is a heading formatted with a standard Heading style—Heading 1, Heading 2, or such. Remember, though, that using such styles will let the Kindle hijack your formatting. So, it's a choice you'll have to make.

To link to a standard heading, select the text you want linked and then Insert Hyperlink—the same as for an external link—but go to the Document tab instead. Click the Locate button next to the Anchor field, then select the heading from the list offered.

If your destination is *not* a standard heading, you'll first have to Insert Bookmark at your destination. Do this with your cursor placed at the beginning of the destination text. Selecting that text will also work but is not necessary.

You can name each bookmark as you like, but with some limitations. The name must start with a letter and must not include any spaces or any punctuation except underscores (_). Also, don't use the exact heading or other destination text as your bookmark name, as this can confuse Word. For your own convenience, use a name that suggests where the bookmark is located.

Now go back and select your link text and Insert Hyperlink. Then just type your bookmark name into the Anchor field, or else click the "Locate" button and select the bookmark from the list offered. After you exit the dialog, check your link to make sure it works.

As with an external link, you can make changes in the Edit Hyperlink dialog. Right-click or Control-click the linked text and choose Hyperlink > Edit Hyperlink.

Try to avoid including a paragraph mark or Manual Line Break in the text you're linking, as this can cause complications. For instance, if the link extends over two lines of text, you won't be able to edit that text in the Edit Hyperlink dialog. (Instead, you'll have to place your cursor at one end of the link and use an arrow key to reach the text to be changed.) An alternative to including the break would be to separately link both lines to the same destination.

●

To keep track of bookmarks you insert, you can go into Word's View options and choose to display bookmarks within the document. Their position is then marked by what looks like an oversize *I*, though this marker can't be moved or deleted. You can also locate a bookmark by calling up the Insert Bookmark dialog box, selecting a bookmark's name, and clicking "Go To." This will move your cursor to the exact location. The Insert Bookmark dialog is also where a bookmark can be deleted.

When you use the Locate function of Insert Hyperlink for headings, this too inserts bookmarks, but they're hidden. You'll never see them within the document, even if you've chosen to display bookmarks. But you can reveal them in the Insert Bookmark dialog box by checking the "Hidden bookmarks" option. (If it's already checked, you may have to uncheck and recheck it before the bookmarks appear.)

The Insert Bookmark dialog box may also reveal extra, unneeded bookmarks, visible or hidden. These might be bookmarks you added yourself, or ones that Word has inserted for its own functioning without telling you. For example, if all or part of your document comes from an older version of Word, you might see a long list of numbered "OLE_LINK" bookmarks. To be safe, you should delete any bookmark not meant for navigation of your Kindle book.

If you edit around a bookmark—say, to add a manual page break before a heading—make sure you haven't shoved the bookmark out of place. If you have, call up the Insert Bookmark dialog box, select the misplaced bookmark, and delete. You can then reinsert the bookmark where it belongs, or else edit the hyperlink to again locate the heading.

It's usually a good idea to recheck the location of your bookmarks shortly before exporting to HTML, to make sure they haven't moved.

Tables of Contents

There's a great deal of confusion about Kindle tables of contents, and for good reason: There are actually two different kinds, and a Kindle book may have one, both, or neither. (Try to get Amazon to explain that to you!)

The first kind is an *HTML table of contents*, also called *embedded*, *internal*, or *inline*. When you export to HMTL, Word will generate one from a linked table of contents you've constructed on a page of your source document. Creating that table in Word is the subject of this section, while the next one tells how to get a link to your table of contents from the Kindle's Go To menu. *The HTML table of contents is the only kind you can export from Word.*

The second kind is an *NCX table of contents*, also called *logical*. *NCX* stands for "navigation control file for XML" or such, and it is a special type of file included in ebooks. The NCX file can be used to place content items like chapter headings directly onto the Kindle's Go To menu as a shortcut for readers. It can also set jump points for Kindles with physical navigation controllers.

While an NCX table of contents is a nice convenience, you don't really need one, as long as you have the HTML table. But besides that, *there is no way to generate an NCX table with Word alone.* Creating the NCX file requires special ebook software or hand-building in HTML—well beyond the scope of this book. So, if you're trying to keep things simple, I suggest you forget about NCX tables of contents.

There's another reason you might want to ignore them: In late 2013, Amazon began experimenting with adding an

NCX table of contents automatically to books submitted without one. Chapter headings and other phrases might now be added some time *after* publication—and not just by the time the book goes on sale! You might see these items only after deleting a book from your Kindle and downloading it again from the Cloud. (If you see such items in the menu for *this* book, that's how they got there.)

I wish I could tell you more. But at the time I noticed it, I couldn't find anyone at Amazon who could explain it or who even knew what I was talking about!

●

The table of contents you can create within Word for your Kindle book is simply a collection of internal links. After listing your headings, you can construct the links using the same techniques described in the previous section.

In fact, if you're using standard headings, you don't even have to list the headings yourself, because you can instead take advantage of Word's automation. In Word for Windows, use Insert Index and Tables, turning off the option "Show page numbers" and turning on "Use hyperlinks instead of page numbers." Word will then generate the entire table of contents for you, links and all! If you need to update, you can just delete what's there and run the command again.

Unfortunately, the hyperlinks option of this command is missing in Word for the Mac—but you can at least automatically generate the list of headings. After that, convert it to editable text by selecting it all and pressing Command-Shift-F9, then add your hyperlinks manually.

But in case you're curious which method I use, I do it *all* manually. Then I don't have to struggle with the automatic formatting applied by Word.

•

Kindle software sometimes wants to know *exactly* where the table of contents ends, and to find that, it looks for text that *isn't* linked. So, avoid interspersing unlinked text within your table of contents—though characters like spaces and punctuation marks don't seem to be a problem.

Menu Items

The Go To menu lets Kindle users jump to locations like your book's "beginning" or to its table of contents. To enable those menu items, you simply place your cursor at the desired locations in your Word document and insert specially-named bookmarks. For the table of contents, the bookmark must be named "toc". For the book's beginning, it's "start". Both of these must be all lower-case.

●

According to Amazon, the "start" bookmark should be placed where the reader would get into the actual book text—for instance, at the beginning of an introduction or a first chapter. The problem is that the designated location is also where the Kindle automatically opens the book the first time. In other words, it's likely the Kindle user will *never* see anything that comes before.

Think about this. If you place the "start" bookmark in the prescribed position, most people opening your book will never see in it your title, your author name, your publishing name, or anything else you put there. As the author and/or publisher, is that what you want? Of course not!

So, my advice is to move your "start" bookmark to the *real* start of your book—the top of the title page.

But then you run into another problem. Believe it or not, if your "start" bookmark falls in front of your table of contents, *the Kindle converter will move it*. Yessirree, the converter will pick it up and place it *after* that table, wherever it might be.

To my mind, that calls for a radical rethink. So, here's my solution: *Always put your table of contents at the head of the document, before the title page or any other text.* The "start" bookmark can then go right after it. On opening the book the first time, the Kindle user will miss only the table of contents, and will usually know enough to reach that through the Go To menu if needed.

You may well have seen advice in books and on the Web to place your table of contents at the *end* of your book—and one popular app for generating Kindle books even offers that option as a special feature. But I hope you now understand why that is a Very Bad Idea.

•

To save you some grief, I'll warn you right now that testing your Go To menu items may not do you much good. For example, due to numerous bugs, they are unlikely to work right or at all in files generated or even just viewed with Amazon's desktop Kindle Previewer. Your best bet is to test on a hardware Kindle with a preview copy converted on the Amazon KDP site.

But even if you get everything to test perfectly, it may mean nothing, because *Amazon KDP staff may manually change the "start" location after publication.* Yes, they may simply move it where they think it *should* be, and without telling you! (As far-fetched as this sounds, it is not speculation. KDP staff will confirm it themselves, if you ask them—as I have.)

The only way to know if this has happened is to get a copy *after* the book has gone on sale. If you discover a change at that point, all you can do is ask KDP staff to change it back—in the hope they'll comply—or else submit your book file again—in the hope it will be treated better the next time. But on the Kindle as in life, there are no guarantees.

Knowing that some hurried, harried KDP staffer may move my "start" location with little care about the consequences, I've taken to indicating a fallback position as clearly as possible. If I'm not allowed to start on the title page, I want to at least not skip any introduction I've added before the first chapter. So, I name this introduction "Getting Started" or even just repeat the book title. Hopefully, no one at Amazon will miss so broad a hint.

5
Final Steps

HTML Export

With your document ready, it's time to tell Word to save your finished text as HTML, the basic language of Web pages and ebooks. The exported file is what you'll submit to Amazon KDP for conversion to your Kindle book.

And, yes, *you do need to export to HTML.* That's despite Amazon's acceptance of Word documents, and despite advice you might find in Kindle formatting "bibles" and the like. One reason I know is that I hear from people who follow most of my instructions but skip this vital step and then complain that their book didn't come out right.

Well, it won't. For best results, you need to control as many steps in the process as you can, not hand them off to Amazon.

●

You will hear over and over how bloated and corrupt Word's exported HTML is, and how long it takes to alter and clean up before submission. One wonders whether the people who claim this are ignorant of HTML, or Word, or Kindle conversion, or all three. Yes, there's some excess in Word's HTML—especially if you don't choose the *correct* export option—but it's not really significant and gives the Kindle converter no problem at all. In fact, the converter has apparently been optimized for Word's HTML!

And, yes, you can spend a fair amount of effort adjusting the code. But that's to overcome problems with the Kindle, not problems with the HTML. Word's code itself—again, when exported with the *right* option—is nearly error-free and easily correctable. And even when not corrected, the few existing errors are ignored by the Kindle converter—which then introduces masses of HTML errors of its own!

In other words, when formatting for Kindle, the faults of Word's HTML are the least of your worries.

•

Before exporting to HTML, *make sure your document is saved.* If you do not save your changes, they'll be in the exported HTML but *not* in your original document. And as I said before, Mac users should beware: If your only change has been to a style definition, you must change something else besides—even if it's only adding then deleting a space—or the Save command won't operate!

The procedure for exporting to HTML will vary according to your version of Word, but you'll be saving as "HTML" or "Web Page" or the like. In the dialog box that comes up, you then want to specify the variety that includes the *least* code. This may be designated as "Web Page, Filtered" or by an option like "Save only display info into HTML." In either case, you'll be choosing to omit code that isn't proper HTML and that could be used only by Word in reimporting the document.

If in doubt about which option to choose, save in alternate ways, then choose the one that creates the *smallest* file. Also, when saving the best way, you should *not* see any auxiliary files with the .xml extension. As still another way to tell, open the file in a text editor. At the very beginning, you should see a plain opening HTML tag (<html>) followed by a head tag (<head>). If you see additional code within and following the opening HTML tag, you've chosen the wrong option.

When saving as HTML, Word may give you a warning about the document losing some formatting if you proceed. Just go ahead with it.

After export, Word will normally open and show you the new HTML document, but translated *back* to Word format for screen display. I suggest you immediately close this to avoid confusing it with your original document. No changes you make to this version will be saved to the original!

•

Word offers a number of "Web Options" related to HTML export. Most of the defaults are fine—and when they aren't, changing them may have no effect anyway!

If you'd like to know, though, the default text encoding for HTML from Word for Windows is "Western European (Windows)," also known as Windows-1252—an encoding that's close but not identical to "Latin-1," officially known as ISO 8859-1. For the Mac, the default is "Unicode (UTF-8)"— which also happens to be the basic encoding of the Kindle. But as I mentioned before, either encoding is handled just fine by the Kindle converter.

By the way, checking the option "Always save Web pages in the default encoding" will mean that Word *ignores* any encoding choice you've made!

•

If you have pictures inside your book, Word will export both an HTML file and a separate pictures folder with an associated name. Before sending all this to Amazon KDP, you'll need to combine it into a single Zip archive. *Do not move your picture files outside of the folder or rename it*. If you do, Word's HTML links to them won't work, and the

Kindle converter won't know where to find them! Instead, include the entire folder in the archive.

On Windows, select both the file and the folder, then right-click and choose "Send to compressed (zipped) folder." Or you can zip just the HTML file and then add the pictures folder to the archive. On the Mac, select file and folder, then Control-click and use the Compress command; or find that command on the File menu.

•

In the early days of Kindle, the simplicity of the Mobipocket format and of the original Kindle hardware made Kindle books a near-perfect candidate for control by Word formatting. But with the introduction of Kindle Format 8 and the proliferation of Kindle models, that has become less and less true.

At this point, I would say that the techniques I describe in this book can bring you about 80% of the way to a well-formatted Kindle book. *And for most readers—and most publishers—that will be enough.* In fact, most Kindle books seem to coast along at well below 80%. (If you don't believe me, just look at the shoddiness of most books about Kindle formatting!)

If you're a perfectionist like me, though, you'll want to tackle that extra 20%. And when working with Word, that involves editing its exported HTML.

An entire book could be written about that, and I've written it: *HTML Fixes for Kindle*. If you're technically inclined and would like to go beyond what this book can offer, get that one. It describes not only a number of refinements you can make to your HTML but also how to automate them so you can process an entire file in literally seconds.

Here are some of the things you can accomplish through changes in HTML that you can't do in Word.

• Adjust bookmarks so headings always retain proper formatting when jumped to.

• Remove all settings that stop the user from choosing their own.

• Keep fonts from appearing much too small or much too large on some Kindles when the book is first opened.

• Make sure indents and other spacing stays relative to larger and smaller font sizes.

• Further guard against the Kindle applying its own defaults in place of your settings.

If you don't want to get that far into technical matters, don't worry about it. Just be ready to accept the occasional quirk of Kindle formatting. You'll have to do *some* of that anyway!

Oh, there's one more benefit of directly editing the HTML. For most books—with little or no additional change—the Kindle-optimized HTML file can easily be converted to EPUB for sale on the iBookstore, Nook, Kobo, and elsewhere. If you want to produce a file for those markets with minimal extra hassle, this is one good approach.

Book Covers

Besides the file or files for your book interior, you'll need an image for your book cover. You'll produce and submit this *separately* from the rest, and then Amazon will merge it into the book as well as use it on the book's Amazon page. *Do not try to add the cover to the book yourself.*

Amazon KDP actually offers an online Cover Creator you can use when submitting your book. To produce a cover beforehand on your computer, you'll need software that can produce either a JPEG or a TIFF, the two picture formats that Amazon accepts. Typically, that might be a photo editor, illustrator program, or page layout program.

Though Word cannot convert its pages to either of those two formats, you can still use it for your layout, if you like. Create the cover in a separate document with zero margins and the page dimension ratio you want. Then export to PDF. To do that in Windows, go to File > Save As, and choose "PDF" as the Save as Type. On the Mac, go to File > Print, and choose "Save as PDF" from the PDF menu.

Once you have the cover in PDF, you can import it into one of the kinds of programs mentioned before and export to JPEG or TIFF. Or do the same after opening it in an advanced PDF reader like Adobe Acrobat or the Mac's Preview.

You'll find further tips on book covers in *Pictures on Kindle*.

●

When exporting to PDF—unlike when exporting to HTML—you don't have to worry about matching a picture's resolution to Word's default of 72 or 96 ppi for the Web. But with recent Word versions, you still need to watch out for resolution changes that Word might impose.

For example, Word 2007 and 2008 won't export pictures at a resolution higher than 220 ppi. Word 2010 and 2011 are better but may still lower the resolution unless you tell them *not* to. To do that in Word 2010 for Windows, go to File > Options > Advanced > Image Size and Quality, then check the option "Do not compress images in file." In Word 2011 for the Mac, go to File > Reduce File Size, then select "Keep current resolution."

Book Data

Besides your book files, it's best to prepare beforehand the information you'll need to set up your book. Here are some notes on what you might need to provide.

Book name. This is your title *without* the subtitle. On some Kindles, the name will be used as a header on each "page" of your Kindle book.

Subtitle. This is optional but often invaluable in helping your book show up in search results. Your combined book name and subtitle can go up to 200 characters. Any more than that, and the name will appear on Amazon with a middle portion cut out, replaced by an ellipsis.

Edition and series info. If needed.

Publisher. This is either your publishing business or an *imprint*—the publishing name for a subset of your books. If you leave it out, Amazon will identify itself as the publisher!

Description. You get 4,000 characters for anything about your book—an actual description, an author bio, testimonials and reviews, an excerpt, a table of contents—in any combination. This will appear near the top of the book's Amazon page.

Book contributors. Author and any other, the way you want the names to appear.

Publication date. This can be the current date or any date *earlier*. You cannot set a date in the future or use this in any way to schedule sales. If you don't want your book placed on sale yet, *don't complete the publishing process.* Amazon allows you to save whatever you've done as a draft and finish later.

ISBN. The International Standard Book Number is what's used to identify books in the book business. A different ISBN is assigned to each book in each format in each edition. At least, that's how it works for *print* books and how you may be *told* it works for ebooks. But in common practice, a book might be given the same ISBN for *all* ebook formats together—and in fact, an ebook doesn't really need an ISBN at all. Amazon allows you to enter an ISBN as an extra point of information about the book but does *not* require one and does *not* use it for identification.

Categories. Amazon asks you to pick one or two categories to help classify your book. It's important to understand that the choices you're offered are *not* Amazon categories! Instead, they're industry-standard categories from a scheme known as the BISAC Subject Headings List. These headings are *mapped* by Amazon to categories in its own ever-evolving hierarchy.

You can browse through BISAC headings at the Web site of the Book Industry Study Group. Keep in mind, though, that the list is tweaked and reissued each year, and the one at KDP may not be up to date.

www.bisg.org

You'll get best results by choosing the most *specific* categories that apply. Amazon will display your book not only in similarly narrow categories but also in all "parent" categories higher up in the hierarchy. So, the further you narrow your category, you more exposure your book may get. Also, your book is more likely to stand out in a narrower category than in a broader one.

It's possible to bypass BISAC entirely by sending KDP a request to enter your book directly into specific Amazon categories. The downside is that any future changes must also go through KDP staff, so you lose the flexibility you might want in experimenting with different choices. Also, if Amazon shifts, splits, or removes a category that your book appears in, the book may be less likely to migrate properly.

Keywords. You can enter up to seven keyword *phrases*, separated by commas. You'll want to provide any likely search terms that didn't make it into your title or description. Besides that, certain standard keywords are used to trigger Amazon's placement of books in categories narrower than those addressed by BISAC. For example, the keywords "baby," "preschool," "ages 6-8," and "preteen" can get your book categorized for specific age categories of children's books. For a full list of such keywords, see this KDP Help page:

kdp.amazon.com/help?topicId=A200PDGPEIQX41

•

Here are a few more general notes for preparing book data for KDP:

• To avoid browser problems, don't use the special characters of book typography. Use standard keyboard characters only! For example, all quotes should be straight, not curly, and dashes should be replaced by double hyphens with space before and after.

In fact, you're better off not keeping your book data in Word at all. A better choice is a text editor like Notepad on Windows, or TextEdit on the Mac. (In TextEdit's

Preferences, make sure you choose "Plain text" as the format and turn off "Smart quotes.") Save your file as "UTF-8" or "UTF-8, no BOM."

• To improve accuracy, avoid retyping book data. Whenever possible, copy the data and paste directly into your browser.

• All the book data you enter at KDP can be changed later—including title and ISBN! (Don't try that with CreateSpace!)

• If you want Amazon to link your Kindle book to a print edition, make sure the Kindle book's title, contributor names, and other basic data exactly match the other edition's. Once the editions are linked, though, you can change that data as you like. (If Amazon hasn't linked them within a few days, request it at Author Central.)

• If you later change the book name, you must click "Save as Draft" before uploading a new file. Otherwise, the inserted header may still be the old title.

•

A number of Kindle authors have taken to fancifying their book descriptions with HTML to make them look more impressive and professional, and also to play tricks with inserting off-site elements. Amazon has now clamped down on some of this, but at the same time, it has released a list of HTML tags for approved use. You can find it here:

kdp.amazon.com/help?topicId=A377RPHW6ZG4D8

But you don't *need* to add HTML at all—you can just stick to normal text. There's only one problem: If you enter more than one paragraph like that, Amazon will ignore any blank lines between them, jamming the paragraphs against each other. My own solution is to add to each blank line a nonbreaking space—Option-8 on my Mac. (That's in a file saved as UTF-8.)

Personally, I don't feel it's worth spending much effort on the *appearance* of the description. That's because, at least on Amazon in the U.S., *only the very top of the description is shown, and the rest is hidden*. Amazon's customers must click a link to see the rest—and of course, most never will.

In any case, I like to *replace* my KDP description on Amazon in the U.S. with descriptive data submitted to Author Central, where most of those same HTML tags are *not* supported. The advantage is that Author Central enables me to claim greatly expanded real estate on the Amazon book page—most of it *not* hidden—and to update my data more quickly—sometimes within minutes, as opposed to days.

Only Author Central in the U.S. provides this ability, but authors from any country may sign up. Find it here:

authorcentral.amazon.com

Submitting and Previewing

When you're ready to test your HTML file, head to Amazon's Kindle Direct Publishing at

kdp.amazon.com

Once you've signed up and started your book setup, you can upload and convert your HTML file and cover image.

•

After conversion, KDP will let you preview your Kindle book either online or on your computer. You can upload and preview as many times as you like, and spend as long as you want doing it. So, take the time to test your Kindle book thoroughly and make any needed changes.

The Kindle Previewer that you can download for offline testing is trickier to run and use, but it's also quicker and in some ways more accurate. In either case, the previewer's Device menu lets you choose different Kindle models for emulation, so you can make sure your formatting works on any of them. Make sure you take advantage of this, as there are major differences between models. Also be sure to switch to Night mode to see if anything disappears.

Of course, the best way to preview a Kindle book is on actual Kindles. You can easily send a preview file as a document to one or more of them with Amazon's Send to Kindle app.

www.amazon.com/sendtokindle

Previewing for Kindle is a large topic in itself. To read much more about it, see my article at

www.newselfpublishing.com/ProofingKindle.html

•

If previewing shows that you need to make changes, do *not* make them in the HTML file—or at least not *just* in there. Go back to your Word document and make them in that. You want to maintain that document as a source that you can easily change at any time and then convert again quickly.

In Amazon KDP's Help pages, you may find advice to instead make all changes in your HTML file. Ignore this. Someone at Amazon got *really* confused.

•

When you're happy with your book's preview, Amazon will ask you to make a few decisions about price, royalty plan, KDP marketing programs, and the like. Then you'll hit "Publish," and your book should start to show up in Kindle stores worldwide in just a day or so.

Congratulations! You're on Kindle!

MORE BOOKS FOR YOU

<u>Pictures on Kindle</u>
Self Publishing Your Kindle Book with Photos,
Paintings, Drawings, and Other Graphics, or Tips on
Formatting Your Images So Your Ebook Doesn't
Look Horrible (Like Everyone Else's)

By Aaron Shepard

HTML Fixes for Kindle
Advanced Self Publishing for Kindle Books, or Tips
on Tinkering with HTML from Microsoft Word or
Anything Else So Your Ebook Looks as Good as It
Possibly Can

By Aaron Shepard

The Business of Writing for Children
An Award-Winning Author's Tips on Writing
Children's Books and Publishing Them, or How to
Write, Publish, and Promote a Book for Kids

By Aaron Shepard

Aaron Shepard's
<u>Sales Rank Express</u>

Quickly Check Amazon Sales Rank and Much More for Print Books, Kindle Books, and Audiobooks on Amazon Sites in Most Countries with the Premier Sales Rank Checker for Authors, Publishers, and Other Book Creators and Marketers

<u>www.salesrankexpress.com</u>

Made in the USA
San Bernardino, CA
02 August 2015